LOOK 2

A Reading Anthology for Young Learners

LUCY CRICHTON

NATIONAL GEOGRAPHIC
LEARNING

Australia • Brazil • Mexico • Singapore • United Kingdom • United States

Contents

STORY 1

The Culture House

Hi! I'm Ella.

This is The Culture House in Copenhagen. It's a community center where you can take a lot of different classes.

The building is really cool.
Let me show you.

The first thing you see is the entrance. You can walk up the stairs, or you can go rock climbing. It's a lot of fun!

Children come here to learn about a lot of different subjects like music, drama, and art.

These are my friends. We come here on Tuesday, Thursday, and Saturday.

I have art on Tuesday. This is the art room. There are a lot of different materials here. You can learn how to make sculptures and collages. My favorite class is painting and drawing.

This is the dance studio. On Friday there are dance classes for young children.

I have gym on Thursday, but on Saturday, when I don't have a class, I come here to sit and dream.

STORY 2

Kind Gardeners

Yusuf and Berat have a garden. This is where they play and work.

Mr. and Mrs. Solack live next door. They're Yusuf and Berat's friends.

The boys knock on the door.

The next day, the boys help in Mr. and Mrs. Solack's garden. They dig up the weeds and water the flowers.

Now the garden is ready.

They all have dinner together.

STORY 3

Different Jobs, Different Faces

In our town, in our town,
A lot of people, up and down.
We live here in Peru,
Can you guess what we do?

Different jobs and different places,
Different clothes and different faces.

He picks you up from where you are,
He drives you up and down.
From your school to the store and home again,
He drives around the town.

Does he see a lot of faces?
Yes, he does, and different places.

He's a taxi driver!

She works with children in our school.
She teaches us to read.
She helps us write, she makes the rules,
It's everything we need!

Does she help you every day?
Yes, she does. We learn and play.

She's a teacher!

He uses stones
To make the walls.
He makes the roof,
The stairs, the doors.

Does he build houses in our town?
Yes, he does. They don't fall down.

He's a builder!

He works outside
In sun and rain.
He grows our food,
Then plants again.

Does he grow beans and peas?
Yes, he does, for you and me.

He's a farmer!

She wears a white coat, she's very kind,
She helps you when in pain.
She gives you the right medicine
And makes you well again!

Does she take good care of you?
Yes, she does. She's there for you.

She's a doctor!

The jobs we do, the jobs we see,
Tell me what you want to be!

STORY
4

The Puppet Show

There's a puppet show today. The puppeteer is getting ready. There are some amazing puppets.

The children are waiting for the show to start. They're talking and laughing.

"The puppets are beautiful! Look! They're wearing colorful costumes."

"What's the story about?" they ask.

The puppeteer just smiles. "Wait and see," he says.

The puppeteer is ready now. The children are watching and listening. They're very excited.

"The story is about an Indian prince and a beautiful princess," says the puppeteer. "The prince wants to find the princess. He goes on a long journey. On the way, the prince helps a tiger in the forest."

"Then the prince finds a magic bed. He flies on the magic bed to the princess. The prince and princess fall in love.

But the king tells the prince he can only marry his daughter if he does some difficult jobs for him."

"The tiger helps him, and the prince marries the princess."

Now the puppets are dancing and singing.

Everyone's watching the story. The children are clapping and laughing. What an amazing puppet show!

STORY 5

Lightning Man

Waru is wise and intelligent. He's an Aboriginal from Australia. He knows all about land, nature, and the weather.

Waru is teaching his grandchildren. He talks about Australia. It's a very big country.

They ask him a lot of questions.

"Why's our land so dry?"

"Yes, Grandpa, it's drier than ever before.
We need rain!"

"Follow me," he says. "Let's go!"

They walk into a forest. It's bigger and darker than any forest they know. They're scared. They stand close to Waru.

He points at the trees. "If the gum trees have flowers, it's windy and dry," he tells them.

"But if the black and red cockatoos are squawking, that means rain isn't far away!"

They walk and walk. Waru stops at a cave.

"Let me show you something," he says.

Inside the cave, there's a painting. "This is Namarrgon, the Lightning Man!" explains Waru.

The children's eyes are open wide.

"Is he making lightning now, Grandpa?"

"Yes, he is."

They go out of the cave. It's windy and it's raining.
They see lightning in the sky.

"The sky is rumbling now. Listen!" says Waru.

"Come on! It's time to pick the plums in the field.
I'm hungry after all of your questions!"

STORY 6

Lion's Teeth

Today there's a costume party in the village.
Zaki is wearing a lion costume. He's late!

A little boy is waiting for the bus with his mom.

Zaki arrives at the bus stop.

"When does the next bus come?" Zaki asks.

The little boy is scared. He doesn't like the lion.

"It comes at nine o'clock," he says.

The bus arrives. It's full of children on the way to the costume party.

There are two crocodiles, three monkeys, two tigers, a zebra, an elephant, and a giraffe on the bus.

The little boy, his mom, and the lion get on.

The little boy sits next to
the giraffe. He doesn't
want to sit next to the lion.
His teeth are too sharp.

Then the bus stops again. A little girl gets on.

"The bus is full!" says the driver.

"There's a place next to me," says the lion.

The little girl sits next to the lion. She's really scared, too. Look at his big, white teeth!

"Look! Don't be scared. I don't have big teeth really!" says Zaki. "I'm missing two teeth!"

The little girl laughs. Everyone on the bus laughs, too!

STORY 1 The Culture House

Look and answer.

Ella's schedule 

Monday	Tuesday	Wednesday	Thursday	Friday	Saturday
	art		gym		music

Felix's schedule 

Monday	Tuesday	Wednesday	Thursday	Friday	Saturday
		computers		dance	art

1. Does Ella have music on Saturday?

Yes, she does.

2. Does Felix have computers on Tuesday?

____

3. Does Ella have art on Monday?

____

4. Does Felix have dance on Friday?

____

5. Does Ella have gym on Thursday?

____

STORY 2

Kind Gardeners

Look and write *We have* or *We don't have*.

1. We have ____________ carrots.
2. ____________ onions.
3. ____________ beans.
4. ____________ tomatoes.
5. ____________ potatoes.
6. ____________ peas.

STORY 3 Different Jobs, Different Faces

Look and answer.

1. Does he build houses?

No, he doesn't.

2. Does she teach us to read?

____

3. Does he grow our food?

____

4. Does he work inside?

____

5. Does she help you?

____

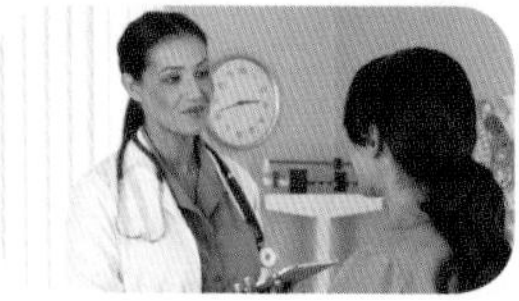

Tell me what you want to be!

I want to be a ______________________.

STORY 4 The Puppet Show

Look and write *A* or *B*.

A

B

1. She's laughing. A
2. He's clapping. ☐
3. She's dancing. ☐
4. He's singing. ☐
5. He's eating cake. ☐
6. She's watching a puppet show. ☐

STORY 5

Lightning Man

Read and complete. Look and answer.

snowing   cloudy   windy   ~~cold~~   sunny   raining

1. Is it 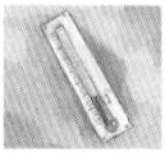 cold ? No, it isn't.

2. Is it  ________ ? ________

3. Is it  ________ ? ________

4. Is it  ________ ? ________

5. Is it  ________ ? ________

6. Is it  ________ ? ________

STORY 6

Lion's Teeth

Look and complete.

tooth ~~bus~~ children buses teeth child

1. Here comes the bus.

2. There's a ______________ at the bus stop.

3. I'm missing two ______________!

4. There are three ______________ on the bus today.

5. I can see two ______________.

6. My little sister only has one ______________!

NATIONAL GEOGRAPHIC
LEARNING

National Geographic Learning,
a Cengage Company

Look 2: A Reading Anthology for Young Learners
Lucy Crichton

Publisher: Sherrise Roehr
Executive Editor: Eugenia Corbo
Publishing Consultant: Karen Spiller
Senior Development Editor: Mary Whittemore
Associate Development Editor: Jen Williams-Rapa
Director of Global Marketing: Ian Martin
Heads of Strategic Marketing:
Charlotte Ellis (Europe, Middle East and Africa)
Kiel Hamm (Asia)
Irina Pereyra (Latin America)
Product Marketing Manager: David Spain
Senior Director of Production: Michael Burggren
Senior Content Project Manager: Nick Ventullo
Media Researchers: Leila Hishmeh, Jeff Millies
Art Director: Brenda Carmichael
Manufacturing Planner: Mary Beth Hennebury
Composition: SPi Global

ISBN: 978-0-357-02752-3

National Geographic Learning
20 Channel Center Street
Boston, MA 02210
USA

Locate your local office at **international.cengage.com/region**

Visit National Geographic Learning online at **ELTNGL.com**
Visit our corporate website at **www.cengage.com**

Credits

Cover: © bauhaus1000/Getty Images.

Photos: 3 © Jens Markus Lindhe; **4** © Torben Eskerod Photography; **5** © Torben Eskerod Photography; **6** © Torben Eskerod Photography; **7** © Torben Eskerod Photography; **8** © Jens Markus Lindhe; **15** (l) © aesthetica/Shutterstock.com; **15** (m) © Anton_Ivanov/Shutterstock.com; **15** (r) © Christian Vinces/Shutterstock.com; **16** Felix Lipov/Alamy Stock Photo; **17** Hemis/Alamy Stock Photo; **18** © Galen Rowell/Getty Images; **19** © andresr/Getty Images; **20** © Rocketclips, Inc./Shutterstock.com; **21** © Santhosh Varghese/Shutterstock.com; **22** © hadynyah/Getty Images; **23** © Dinodia Photo/Getty Images; **24** Travel Pictures/Alamy Stock Photo; **25** dave stamboulis/Alamy Stock Photo; **26** Dinodia Photos/Alamy Stock Photo; **42** (t, b) © Olga1818/Shutterstock.ocm; **44** (t) Felix Lipov/Alamy Stock Photo; **44** (mt) Hemis/Alamy Stock Photo; **44** (m) © Galen Rowell/Getty Images; **44** (mb) © andresr/Getty Images; **44** (b) © Rocketclips, Inc./Shutterstock.com.

Illustrations: 9–14, 43 Yulia Pietetskaya/Advocate Art; **27-34, 46** Gerald Kelly/Painted Words; **35–41, 47** Veronica Montoya/Advocate Art; **45** Rayanne Viera/Bright group.

Printed in China
Print Number: 08 Print Year: 2023